Aglee the Eaglet

Chelsea Kong

© 2021-2024 Chelsea Kong

All rights reserved. All images used in this book are licensed copies from their respectful owners including myself, Jasmine, Canva, Freepik, Pixabay, Pexels, and Unsplash. This book or any portion thereof may not be reproduced or used in any manner whatsoever without the express written permission of the publisher except for the use of brief quotations in a book review.

Printed in 2023, Made in Toronto, Canada
ISBN: 978-1-990399-60-2
Library and Archives Canada

Hello, readers! Have you heard of Aglee the Eagle?

Aglee welcomes you to her story. Do you know that eagles soar rather than fly? Yes, unlike other birds, eagles use the wind to help them to soar rather than using their wings to fly. Eagles are also large, but this story is about an eaglet that is learning to become an eagle.

Aglee lives in a nest high on the mountaintop with her father, mother, sister, and brother. She is the oldest of the eaglets. A beautiful view of the land below and the perfect blue sky. She could see everything from there. She loved being high on the mountain.

Aglee's father told Aglee's mom that he will be back with the food.

Father said, "I will be back with the food. Stay with your mother until I come back."

Aglee asked, "Dad, when can I learn to soar like you?"

Father said, "When you are ready. You need to let your wings grow more and get stronger to stay above the wind. You need to sharpen your beak and claws every day."

Aglee said, "It must be nice to soar and feel the wind."

Father said, "Yes. One day you will get to soar, but today just stay with your mom. It's safer for you."

Aglee did what her father said, and she went back to her family.

Mom was making sure that her sister and brother were safe.

Aglee asked, "Mom, do you know when I can learn to soar like you and Dad?"

Mom said, "Aglee, when I was young, I also wanted to soar. My father said, "It takes time to be good at soaring. First, your wings need to grow long enough and be strong. You need to be able to stay on the wind. The wind helps you to soar."

Aglee said, "Did you have to wait long?"

Mom said, "Yes. It takes time for the wings to grow and to make your beak and claws sharp and strong."

Aglee want to soar like her parents, but she knew that she had to wait.

Mom said, "Aglee, why don't you talk to your sister and brother for now? Father will be back with the food. I am going to stretch my wings, but I am keeping watch. "

Aglee went to her sister and brother. The two eaglets were playing chase.

Aglee, do you want to play chase?" asked Eglea.

Aglee said, "Okay. Let's have fun together."

The wind started to blow after they played for a while. Aglee, her sister, and her brother saw it was getting windy.

"OH, NO!" SAID EGLEA.

MOM EAGLE SAID, "COME INTO THE NEST AGLEE, EGLEA, AND ALEGE."

THE THREE EAGLETS WERE RUNNING AS FAST AS THEY COULD, BUT THE WIND WAS GETTING CLOSER TO THEM.

MOM EAGLE HAD TO DO SOMETHING FAST. SHE SPREAD OUT HER WINGS AND THE THREE EAGLETS TRIED TO HIDE UNDER
HER WINGS.

AGLEE SAW THAT HER BROTHER ALEGE HAD TRIPPED ON A ROCK, AND SHE RAN TO HIM AS FAST AS SHE COULD.

HER SISTER ELEGA GOT SAFE UNDER MOM. MOM KNEW THAT IF SHE DID NOT GET THEM TO SAFETY, THEY WILL BE IN DANGER. SHE HAD TO KEEP EGLEA UNDER HER WHILE GOING TO THE OTHER EAGLETS.

"EGLEA, STAY CLOSE TO ME WHILE I HELP YOUR SISTER AND BROTHER," SAID MOM.

MOM RAN WITH EGLEA, TRYING TO STAY UNDER HER. SHE REACHED AGLEE AND ALEGE.

MOM SAID, "WE NEED TO STAY TOGETHER."

The four of them stayed close to get back to the nest. They made it back safely.

"That was close," said Alege.

"Yes, how did you trip on the way?" asked Aglee.

"I was running as mom said and didn't see the rock," said Alege.

"It's good that you didn't get blown by the wind since we can't soar yet," said Eglea.

"How would we get up if we fell?" asked Alege.

"If I could soar, then I can help," said Aglee.

"Yes, I could also help too," said Eglea.

"One day, you all be able to soar, but for now you have to wait and stay safe in the nest when the wind comes," said mom.

The wind started to slow down and go away.

"Now, it's safe again," said mom.

Aglee, Eglea, and Alege came out of the nest. Father Eagle came back with fish under his feet for the family and he dropped them near the nest.

Father Eagle comes to bring more food for the eaglets. Eaglets eat 8 times a day.

"Come Aglee, Alege, and Eglea. It's time to eat lunch!," said Father Eagle.

The three came to see the fish Father brought. He brought back three big fish.

"The three of you are going to share the one fish. There is enough food there for you three to eat," said Father.

Father was right. The three eaglets had plenty to eat from the one big fish that their father gave them.

"It was windy earlier and Alege tripped. Aglee went to go help her brother. I had to rush and keep Eglea under my wings, but we got back to the nest safely," said Mom.

"It's good that you did. I also saw and felt that it got windy. I had to wait since I got the fish and had to keep it safe," said Father.

"Yes," said Mom.

"We just need to make sure that the wind doesn't get stronger," said Father.

Father Eagle looked around to make sure that things were clear from the wind. He wanted to keep the eaglets safe. He looked around at the rock that Alege tripped on and to see if he could move it away. He picked up the rock with his talons and then flew away to drop it a way where the eaglets would not fall on it again. Then he came back and looked for anything else he could find that would be dangerous.

The three eaglets started to play again. Then the sun started to come out again.

"Look! The sun is coming back out again," said Aglee.

"Then there should be no more wind", said Eglea.

"That's good. I want the sun to stay," said Alege.

"Dad, got rid of the rock that you tripped on," said Aglee.

"Yes, he did, but I still want the sun," said Alege.

"It's a lot warmer when it's not windy and better to play in. I also like the sun more than the wind," said Eglea.

"The wind is good for soaring," said Aglee.

"Dad said we have to wait," said Eglea.

"It seems like it will be a long time before we can soar," said Alege.

"I guess we can start to make our wings, claws, and beaks stronger," said Aglee.

"That's a great idea!" shouted Eglea.

"Yes! We can do that!" shouted Alege.

"Let's play it as a game too," said Aglee.

Yes, we can find something like the rock," said Alege.

"We need to find another one," said Eglea.

"Maybe we can use the tree for now," said Aglee.

"That will work too," said Eglea.

A stranger eagle and his mother came to where the three eaglets were.

He and his mother have their fish food to eat separately from the eaglets. After they did, father and mother go perch in the trees watching the three.

Aglee goes and pecks with her beak against the tree, trying once again to get her beak stronger. Her siblings also pecking away to work their beaks to get stronger.

"What are you doing?" said an unfamiliar voice.

Aglee looks to see in the distance to see another eagle that was older than her.

"I am trying to make my beak stronger," said Aglee.

"Why are trying to use the tree to do that? Don't you know you need to be careful?" said the eagle.

"Yes. I understand," said Aglee.

"If you can't soar yet, then it's hard once you fall," said the eagle.

"How do you know that?" asked Aglee.

"I AM OLDER THAN YOU. I CAN TELL YOU DON'T KNOW HOW TO SOAR YET. I CAN SEE YOUR PARENTS ARE WATCHING YOU FROM A DISTANCE," SAID THE EAGLE.

"You are a stranger," said Aglee.

"Yes. I know that you want to learn to soar," he said.

"Are you watching me?" asked Aglee.

"I have seen you from such a distance," he said and asked, "why do you want to soar so badly?"

"Soaring is great! I like to have the wind under my wings and explore what is out there, but why are you asking?" said Aglee.

"Well, if you want to learn to soar, you have to learn to use your wings. I can see you are so eager to soar and thought to tell you," the eagle said.

"My father and mother told me that I need to make my beak strong and claws sharp, too," she said.

"That is part of the steps to soar. If you don't even know how to use your wings, then you can't do much. You need to learn fast how to do it too," he said.

"Why are you telling me this?" she asked.
"I know how you can soar,

But the way you are doing it is not right," he said.

"What is your idea?" Aglee asked.

"You need to learn to spread out your wings and feel the wind under them and take a step out to let it lift you. You need to be able to sync with the wind if you want to soar," he said.

"Thank you for the advice," Aglee said.

"You're welcome. That's how I learned to soar," he said.

"Who taught you?" Aglee asked.

"I learned it by watching my father and listening to him tell me to open up my wings and ride on the wind. You can't be afraid of falling when you soar or you won't make it," he said.

"Really?" asked Aglee.

"Yes, if you are too scared, you can't soar. You need to have the courage to do it," he said.

"I will think about it," said Aglee.

Then she went back towards her sister and brother, who were still pecking their beaks.

"Alege and Eglea, some eagle just told me that we are trying to learn to soar all wrong," said Aglee.

"Who told you that?" asked Eglea

"Why is a stranger trying to tell you how to soar?" asked Alege.

"He said that knows that I want to soar," said Aglee.

"It seems that this stranger is watching," said Alege.

"Yes, that's what I was thinking too," said Aglee.

"He shouldn't be watching us," said Eglea.

"What about father and mother? I am sure that they are watching all the time?" said Alege

"Yes, they are watching us from a distance," said Eglea.

"I think we should ask them about what the eagle said. After all, he is a stranger," said Alege.

"I am not sure if it's a good idea to listen to a stranger, Aglee," said Eglea.

"I ALSO THINK I SHOULD ASK WHAT FATHER AND MOTHER THINK," SAID AGLEE.

THE THREE EAGLETS THEN CALLED TO THEIR PARENTS, "FATHER AND MOTHER!"

Father and Mother Eagle heard them.

"What is it, you three?" asked Father Eagle.

"A stranger told me that to soar I need to open my wings and to ride on the wind," said Aglee.

"That may be true. You need to feel the wind and know how to use it to help you move forward and soar," said Father Eagle.

"Why is that stranger talking to you?" asked Mother Eagle.

"He said he knows that I want to soar. I think he just wanted to help," said Aglee.

"Some strangers you need to be careful about," said Mother Eagle.

"You do need to watch out for strangers. Sometimes they can pretend to be friends," said Father Eagle.
"I understand," said Aglee.

"Just be careful about strangers. You can learn to soar, but you need to be very careful right now," said Mother Eagle.

"WE KNOW IT'S NOT EASY FOR YOU TO WAIT, BUT WE KNOW WHAT IS BEST," SAID FATHER EAGLE.

"ONE DAY I DO WANT TO SOAR JUST LIKE YOU AND MOTHER," SAID AGLEE.

"IT WILL HAPPEN ONE DAY. I WILL BE BACK AGAIN LATER," SAID FATHER EAGLE AS HE FLEW AWAY.

THEN ONE DAY CAME AS WEEKS PASSED BY. AGLEE'S WINGS GREW BIGGER AND STRONGER AND LONGER. SHE WAS NOW OLDER. SHE AND HER SIBLINGS WERE NOW 1/2 YEARS OLD.

"IT'S TIME TO TRY TO SOAR," SAID AGLEE TO HERSELF.

AGLEE'S FATHER AND MOTHER KNEW THAT IT'S TIME FOR HER TO START TRYING TO LEARN TO SOAR.

"AGLEE, OPEN YOUR WINGS WIDE AND BELIEVE AND FEEL THE WIND UNDER YOUR WINGS," SAID FATHER EAGLE.

"KEEP YOUR EYES LOOKING FORWARD WHEN YOU SOAR. YOUR BEAK FORWARD AND FEET DOWN," SAID MOTHER EAGLE.

FATHER SHOWED HOW TO SOAR IN FRONT OF AGLEE. SHE SAW HER FATHER AND THEN HER MOTHER GET OFF THE BRANCH AND SOAR AROUND.

"I can do this," said Aglee and so she tried to lift herself with her wings spread and to feel the wind under her wings.

Aglee began to feel the wind under her wings as she leaped. At first, she had a slight bit of trouble.

"KEEP YOUR WINGS SPREAD," SAID FATHER EAGLE.

AGLEE LISTENED TO HER FATHER'S INSTRUCTIONS AND SPREAD WIDE HER WINGS AS HER PARENTS DID. THEN, BEFORE SHE KNEW IT, SHE BEGAN TO LIFT AND SOAR AS THEY DID. AGLEE WAS AMAZED AND SO HAPPY.

"NOW, YOU KNOW HOW TO SOAR," SAID FATHER EAGLE. "CONGRATULATIONS AGLEE! YOU ARE NOW ARE BECOMING AN EAGLE," SAID MOTHER EAGLE.

ALEGE AND EGLEA SAW AGLEE IN THE AIR, SOARING AROUND. THEY ALSO TRIED TO SPREAD THEIR WINGS BUT WERE NOT ABLE TO CATCH THE WIND, SO FATHER AND MOTHER EAGLE SAVED THEM AND PUT THEM BACK INTO THE TREE.

"YOU ARE NOT READY YET TO SOAR, BUT YOUR TIME WILL ALSO COME," SAID FATHER EAGLE.

"WE WANT TO SOAR TOO," SAID EGLEA.

"HOW LONG DO WE NEED TO WAIT?" ASKED ALEGE.

"JUST WAIT AND SEE UNTIL YOU ARE GROWN JUST A FEW DAYS MORE," SAID MOTHER EAGLE.

"YOU ARE ALMOST READY, BUT NOT QUITE YET," SAID FATHER EAGLE.

"When will I be ready?" asked Aglee who felt sad.

"You are growing stronger every day. Your wings are growing longer. Your beak and talons need to stay sharp and strong too. As an eagle, you will need to learn how to catch food to eat too," Father Eagle said.

"We are proud that you are growing more like an eagle every day," Mother Eagle said.

"How will we know when we are ready?" asked Eglea.

"When your wings are able to master balancing your body but after you learned how to soar for a while you will be able to leave the nest and look for a new home," said Father Eagle.

"When you are ready to leave, you will need to learn how to mate and have eaglets of your own," said Mother Eagle.

"Really? Maybe I am not ready for that," said Aglee. "I like being here with Father and Mother," said Agele.

"You are still young, so you don't need to think about that now," said Father Eagle.

"Then I will just wait. I am not ready to leave the nest. I will miss all of you," said Aglee.

"I will miss you too," said Eglea.

"I also agree," said Alege.

"We will also miss you, so just be patient for the right time," said Mother Eagle.

Aglee agreed with her parents and waited patiently to grow older. Now, she did not want to grow up too fast.

She had been practicing using her wings to soar. She kept trying until she could soar well.

She was able to soar as good as her father and mother and they were proud of her. Her feathers grew longer than before. She flew higher and higher each time she tried. She loves to soar now.

Aglee, Eglea, and Alege grew and grew until they three years old adults and are now ready to leave their home and find a place of their own. Their feathers were now a mix of brown and greyish white with brown body and some orange colour in her tail feathers. As they went on their own, they had to make their nest and then when they are ready, they have to prepare for a mate.

AFTER TIME AGLEE'S FEATHERS CHANGED COLOUR AGAIN. HER HEAD BECAME FULL OF WHITE FEATHERS AND HER BODY WAS BROWN. SHE MADE HERSELF READY FOR HER MATE SO THAT SHE COULD ALSO HAVE A FAMILY OF HER OWN. SHE WOULD BUILD WITH HER MATE IN A HIGH PLACE IN ON THE TOP OF THE MOUNTAIN.

THE END!

It may be the end of the story but there are still more pages to this book. Find facts about eagles and I have another book on eagles that is also great for young children.

INTERESTING FACTS ABOUT EAGLES

Bald eagles are dark brown with their head and tail covered in white feathers. They have yellow beaks; large talons and their feet have small spikes that are called "spicules" to catch food. The young eagles, also called "eaglets," are a light grey colour and their feathers are fluffy after they hatched (Canadian Geographic, Bald Eagles).

They have powerful talons, and they swoop down on their prey at an angle to catch them. They use their hooked beak to pull flesh out before they eat it.

Female eagles are larger than male eagles.
The adult eagles perch on trees away from their eaglets.
Eagles make large nests for their eggs in the tall trees.
Eagles can see from high heights.
The eaglets eat food 8 times a day.
They like high places and mountains.
They live close to the water and eat fish, ducks, snakes, turtles, rabbits, muskrats, and dead animals.
They can go up to 160 km/hour (100 mph) when they dive.

They can climb up to 3000 m (10,000 ft.) in the air. They can soar for hours using these currents. When cruising, they can fly about 65 km/hour (40 mph).

They take a month or two to fly and soar. Eagles return to the area that they were born. They can live for 20-25 years. Eagles talk to each other by making sounds like calls, screams, and whistles.

They sharpen their beaks and talons and pull off their feathers and grow them again. This helps them to grow new feathers that will make them soar higher and faster. It is painful and they need to remain alone. They have to wait for other eagles to give them food to eat. They sharpen their beaks and talons against the rocks.

Eagles choose a mate when they are 4-5 years old through courtship and stay for life except if one dies or disappears, then they look for another. Their nests can weigh up to 900 kg (1 ton). Eaglets have brown feathers after 3 weeks and they learn to soar between 10-12 weeks. (Animal Fact Guide)

BALD EAGLES TURN FROM GREY TO BROWN. THEY ALSO TURN WHITE BEFORE THEY BECOME BROWN AND WHITE AS THEY GROW INTO THEIR ADULT LOOK AND SIZE.

EAGLES LIKE TO LIVE IN A NEW PLACE CLOSE TO WHERE THEY WERE BORN AND GREW INTO AN EAGLET. THAT IS WHERE THEY WILL BUILD A NEST, MATE, AND HAVE THEIR OWN BABY EABLES.

You can learn more about eagles from watching them grow. Some people train eagles and work with them every day.

CHELSEA'S WATER COLOUR PAINTING OF AN EAGLE FLYING BY THE MOUNTAINS.

REFERENCES

Animal Fact Guide and Journey North, "Bald Eagle" North Journey, 1997 - 2019, https://journeynorth.org/tm/eagle/facts_ecology.html

Learn Bird Watching, "How Do Eagles Fly? Revealing the Secrets of Their Soaring." Learn Bird Watching 2023, https://learnbirdwatching.com/how-do-eagles-fly/

Message from the Author

Thank you for taking the time to read this book. Please leave a review for the author after you read this book. It will help the author to write more books. Your support is much appreciated too. I hope you enjoyed it as much as I enjoyed writing it. You can check out more of my books in the next few pages and please help leave a review as it will help get more readers like you to read and also encourages me to write more books. This is my first attempt to writing a story book for school aged children. When I was younger, I also enjoyed telling stories and writing comics with my sister and brother. I hope one day to get more stories published that I have in my heart about superhero adventures.

OTHER PRODUCTS

- Knowing God
- How to Hear God's Voice
- New Life in Jesus
- Loving Israel
- God's Gifts/Spiritual Talents
- Meeting God
- Word Power
- Fruit of the Spirit
- The Tabernacle
- Bride for Jesus
- A Life of Prayer
- Live Free
- Who am I in Jesus
- Walk in Love
- God's Favor
- Man of God
- Woman of God
- How to Use Money
- God's Wisdom
- Fasting
- See Jerusalem and Bethany
- First Fruit Offering
- Feast of Trumpets

- Day of Atonement
- Feast of Tabernacles
- Counting the Omer
- Festival of Lights
- Glory, Presence, and Holy Spirit
- Live in God's Presence
- Pentecost
- See Galilee, Nazareth, and Tiberias
- Hear God Speak
- Knowing Jesus
- Knowing Holy Spirit
- A Healthy Life and Healthy Life Work Book
- Smokey the Cat
- Passover Unleavened Bread
- Resurrection Life
- The Blessing
- Revival
- Chelsea Learns Hebrew
- Thanksgiving
- Give Thanks
- Jesus Birth
- Loving Jesus: Bride and Groom
- Proverbs 31 Woman

OTHER PRODUCTS

ABC of People in the Bible
Colours in the Bible
Breakthroughs
Open Doors
The Seven Spirits of God
Numbers in the Bible
An Eagle's Life
ABC's of Faith

Coming soon

Teaching Series
How to Hear God's Voice Teaching Guide & Audio Book
Relationship with God, Jesus, Holy Spirit Guide
Knowing God, Jesus, Holy Spirit Guide & Audio Book
Flowing in the Prophetic

Teaching (Non-Sale on my website)
Purim
Passover
Resurrection

More books to come!

Devotionals
31 Day Devotional

Inspirational/Other
Chelsea's Psalms and Poems
Your Daily Meal: Chelsea's Photo Album

Puzzle Books
Biblical Puzzle Book Vol 1-5
Bible Puzzles for Young Children Book 1-3
Biblical Puzzle for Children Books 1-5

BOOK REVIEWS

More books on Amazon, Kobo, and Barnes and Noble, Smashwords, and IngramSpark.
https://chelseak532002550.wordpress.com/

More books on Amazon, Kobo, and Barnes and Noble, Smashwords, and IngramSpark.
https://www.amazon.com/author/chelseakong

Please leave a review and share with friends to help the author continue to write more books to reach more readers. Thank you so much for your support.

Review!

About
CHELSEA KONG

She is a writer, creative arts and digital media artist, skilled administration and payroll professional, and podcaster. Chelsea also served in a variety of roles, from audiovisual, photography, to assisting on the worship team, and ministry team. She also has a passion for families being united.

Chelsea has been a guest on Unity Live Radio, The Lady Tracey Show, and How to Live for Christ and is highly recommended by a Proud Christian blog. She is also a guest blogger. A few of her books have been featured in YourAuthorHub, etc. She graduated from Hotel and Restaurant Management, Digital Media Arts, Office Administration, Payroll Professional, and experience working with children. Chelsea lives in Toronto, Canada. She mainly writes children's books, stories, bridal writing, poems, lyrics for songs, words of encouragement, blessings, prayers, and jokes. The author of How to Hear the Voice of God, the Bridal Collection, Knowing God, etc. She also has her own Bible Puzzle books and other inspired products. Her podcast channel is called Chelsea K on Anchor, Spotify, and iTunes.

Please check my website to find out more:
https://chelseak532002550.wordpress.com/

About
JASMINE KONG

She is a self-employed artist in graphics, web, and gaming. She graduated from Tradigital Animation and has studied Graphic Design. She produces her own graphics for commissions. Her graphics range from simple to more complicated. Her favourite art style is anime and she enjoys watching Japanese anime. She also produces graphics suitable for websites. She has also been featured in an anime book and won first prize for the contest. Everyone who knows about her artwork enjoys it. She has even had an opportunity to show students how to do a bit of origami.

www.ingramcontent.com/pod-product-compliance
Lightning Source LLC
Chambersburg PA
CBHW041413010526
44107CB00016B/1156